CAROLS
FOR CHOIRS 5

Fifty Christmas Carols

Edited and arranged by
BOB CHILCOTT & DAVID BLACKWELL

MUSIC DEPARTMENT

OXFORD
UNIVERSITY PRESS

OXFORD
UNIVERSITY PRESS

Great Clarendon Street, Oxford OX2 6DP, England

Oxford University Press is a department of the University of Oxford.
It furthers the University's aim of excellence in research, scholarship,
and education by publishing worldwide in

Oxford New York
Auckland Cape Town Hong Kong Karachi
Kuala Lumpur Madrid Melbourne Mexico City Nairobi
New Delhi Shanghai Taipei Toronto

With offices in

Argentina Austria Brazil Chile Czech Republic France Greece
Guatemala Hungary Italy Japan Poland Portugal Singapore
South Korea Switzerland Thailand Turkey Ukraine Vietnam

Oxford is a registered trade mark of Oxford University Press
in the UK and in certain other countries

3 5 7 9 10 8 6 4

ISBN 978-0-19-337356-3 (paperback)
ISBN 978-0-19-337712-7 (wiro)

Music origination by Katie Johnston
Printed in Great Britain on acid-free paper by
Halstan Ltd, Amersham, Bucks

PUBLISHER'S NOTE

In August 1961, Oxford University Press published a practical, inexpensive new collection of carols and Christmas hymns in choral arrangements, with accessible orchestrations for many of the items available on hire. This book, *Carols for Choirs*, with its green livery and design of an angel on the cover, soon became one of the best-selling carol anthologies of all time. The editors, Reginald Jacques and David Willcocks, ensured that the contents would serve concerts and services equally well, and that familiar repertoire was complemented with items especially written for the collection (four newly composed items were included). One of the book's features was the concept of uniting under one cover all the material that a choir would need for their event, and another was the inclusion of an Order of Service for the benefit of choirs who modelled their services on the Festival of Nine Lessons and Carols at King's College, Cambridge.

Such was the book's success that further volumes followed, with John Rutter joining David Willcocks as fellow series editor (Jacques died in 1969). *Carols for Choirs 2* (1970) again covered a mix of traditional and new, and also included material for an Advent service. *Carols for Choirs 3* (1978) included simpler arrangements, and some unadorned medieval and Baroque items, and *Carols for Choirs 4* (1980) met the demand for an upper-voice collection. The larger compilation *100 Carols for Choirs* (1987) contains items from the first three books, with twenty-six new inclusions. Collectively, the books have enhanced, and in many cases shaped and defined, the Christmas musical experience of many thousands of singers, musicians, and listeners for fifty years: the *Carols for Choirs* series is used by cathedrals and town-square carol-singers, schools and parish churches, and by choral societies and folk simply wishing to enjoy carols in their homes. The publication of *Carols for Choirs 5*, under the editorship of Bob Chilcott and David Blackwell, ensures that the legacy of this well-loved series will be continued for many years to come.

SIMON WRIGHT
Music Department, Oxford University Press
June 2011

PREFACE

It is a great pleasure to have the opportunity to mark the fiftieth anniversary of the first collection in the *Carols for Choirs* series by introducing a fifth volume of carols and arrangements. It is probably fair to say that over the past fifty years the *Carols for Choirs* series has been one of the most important Christmas resources for choir singers and conductors worldwide. It has also been an inspiration to composers and arrangers, giving them the confidence to write new carols, as well as helping singers, congregations, and audiences to embrace the new alongside the more traditional.

Our aim with this publication is to bring to the fore as many new carols and arrangements as we can. Within this volume are forty new carols representing the work of thirty composers and arrangers, not only from the United Kingdom but also from the United States, Canada, Finland, and Switzerland. The remaining ten carols are existing favourites that have been published by Oxford University Press in recent years. We have aimed to include carols and hymns that will find a place not only in a traditional carol service but also within the repertoire of the carol concert, as reflected in the number of orchestral accompaniments that have been made available.

Thanks are due to all the composers who have contributed to this publication, to Robyn Elton for her careful editing, and to Flora Death for all her work on the scores and parts for the carol orchestrations. But perhaps the greatest thanks should go to Reginald Jacques, Sir David Willcocks, and John Rutter, whose inspirational work has enabled the *Carols for Choirs* series to take flight, and given us the energy to carry it forward with confidence.

BOB CHILCOTT AND DAVID BLACKWELL
Oxford
June 2011

INDEX OF TITLES AND FIRST LINES

Where first lines differ from titles, the former are shown in italics.

★ Carols marked with an asterisk may be sung unaccompanied.

The following items may be considered for use at seasons other than Christmas:

Annunciation (*25 March*): I sing of a maiden (p. 73), There is no rose (p. 192 and p. 195)

Advent: Adam lay ybounden (p. 2), I sing of a maiden (p. 73), Lo, how a Rose e'er blooming (p. 102), O come, O come, Emmanuel (p. 115), There is no rose (p. 192 and p. 195), Voices in the Mist (p. 216)

St Stephen (*Boxing Day, 26 December*): Good King Wenceslas (p. 63)

New Year/secular: New Year (p. 108), Old Christmas Returned (p. 127), The Sparrows' Carol (p.182), Wassail (p. 218)

Epiphany (*6 January*): A little child there is yborn (p. 16), Glory to the Christ Child (p. 50), My Lord has Come (p. 105), O come, all ye faithful (p. 132), Out of the orient crystal skies (p. 136), We three kings of Orient are (p. 207), What child is this? (p. 226)

INDEX OF ORCHESTRATIONS AVAILABLE FOR HIRE/RENTAL

The following orchestral accompaniments are available to hire from the publisher's Hire/Rental Library or appropriate agent. Please quote the Hire Index number when ordering material.

Orchestrations are shown numerically to correspond with the traditional layout of an orchestral score, thus '2.1.2.1 – 4.3.3.1 – timp – hp (opt.) – str' indicates an orchestra comprising 2 flutes, 1 oboe, 2 clarinets, 1 bassoon; 4 horns, 3 trumpets, 3 trombones, tuba; timpani, harp (optional), and strings.

CAROL	SCORING	HIRE INDEX NO.
A little child there is yborn	1.1.1.1 – 1.0.0.0 – perc – str	356
Away in a manger (AB)	solo (fl, ob, or vn), hp or pno (opt.), str (db opt.)	357
Away in a manger (BC)	strings	358
Candlelight Carol	fl, ob, hp, str	178
Ding dong! merrily on high †	picc.2.2.2.2 – 4.0.0.0 – timp, 3perc, handbells (opt.) – hp – str	325
God rest you merry, gentlemen	• 2.2.2.2 – 2.1.1(opt.).0 – str	372
	• 2tpt, hn, tbn, tuba, organ	380
Good King Wenceslas	2.2.2.2 – 2.2.0.0 – timp – str	359
Hark! the herald-angels sing	• 2.1.2.1 – 2.2.2.0 [or 2.2.1.1] – timp, perc – str	381
	• 2tpt, hn, tbn, bass tbn or tuba, timp, perc, organ	366
In dulci jubilo	2.2.2.2 – 2.2.0.0 – timp – str	360
It came upon the midnight clear (JS)	• 2.2.2.2 – 4.3.3.1 [or 2.2.3.0] – timp, perc – str	371
	• 2tpt, hn, tbn, tuba	382
It came upon the midnight clear (MW)	2hn, str, organ	374
Joy to the world!	2.2.2.2 – 2.2.0.0 – timp – str	383
New Year	2.1.2.1 – 2.0.0.0 – hp – str	326
O come, all ye faithful	• 2.2.2.2 – 2.2.3.1 [or 2.2.0.0] – timp, perc – str	370
	• 2tpt, hn, tbn, tuba, timp (opt.)	377
O come, O come, Emmanuel	2.1.2.1 – 2.0.0.0 – str	367
O little town	fl, ob, str	361
Scots Nativity	• 2.1.2.1 [or 1.0.1.0] – 2(opt.).0.0.0 – glock (opt.) – hp (opt.) – str	304
	• 2tpt, hn, tbn, tuba	313
See amid the winter's snow	2.1.2.1 – 2.0.0.0 – str	368
Silent night	strings	362
Sussex Carol	2.2.2.2 – 2.0.0.0 – timp, 2perc – str	300
The Bell Carol	fl, cl, bn, glock, str	378
The holly and the ivy	1.1.1.1 – str	384
The Sparrows' Carol	fl, ob, cl, str	363
Wassail	• 1.1.2.1 – 2.2.0.0 – timp (opt.) – str	375
	• 2tpt, hn, tbn, tuba	376
We three kings of Orient are	2.2.2.2 – 2.2.3.1 – timp, perc, pno – str	369
While shepherds watched their flocks	2.2.2.2 – 2.2.0.0 – timp – str	364

† In the orchestrated version of this carol there are extended instrumental interludes at bars 25 and 53.

Commissioned by Matthew Owens for the Choir of St Mary's Episcopal Cathedral, Edinburgh

1. Adam lay ybounden

15th-cent. English

HOWARD SKEMPTON
(b. 1947)

Also available separately (ISBN 978–0–19–343247–5).

2. Away in a manger

19th-cent. American

Melody by W. J. KIRKPATRICK (1838–1921)
arr. ALAN BULLARD (b. 1947)

In verse 1 the altos, tenors, and basses may hum while the sopranos sing the words.

for Christina

3. Away in a manger

19th-cent. American

Melody by JAMES R. MURRAY (1841–1905)
arr. BOB CHILCOTT (b. 1955)

1. A - way in a man - ger, no crib for a bed, The lit - tle Lord Je - sus laid down his sweet head; The stars in the bright sky looked down where he lay, The lit - tle Lord Je - sus a - sleep on the hay.

DESCANT (SOPRANOS)

ALL OTHER VOICES

2. The cat - tle are low - ing, the ba - by a - wakes, But

lit - tle Lord Je - sus no cry - ing he makes. I love thee, Lord Je - sus! Look

down from the sky, And stay by my side un - til morn - ing is nigh.

3. Be_ near me,_ I_ ask_ thee to

3. Be near me, Lord Je - sus; I ask thee to stay Close

Ped.

for Richard Mayo and Dulwich College Chapel Choir

4. A Heavenly Song

15th-cent. English
adap. Rosemary Greentree

CECILIA McDOWALL
(b. 1951)

A heav'n-ly song, I dare well say, Is sung on earth to man_____ this
day. Song, I dare well say, Is_____ sung this

day, this day.

4. He is a lord, and by na-ture A maid-en's breast he

5. A little child there is yborn

Anon. 15th cent.

MALCOLM ARCHER
(b. 1952)

clerk - es sing in their se - quence.

5. Now sit we down u - pon our knee,

Ei - a, ei - a, su - san - ni, And pray we to the Tri - ni-ty, *Al - le -*

6. A Patre Unigenitus

Anon. 15th cent.
adap. and trans. Hugh Keyte and Andrew Parrott

CARL RÜTTI
(b. 1949)

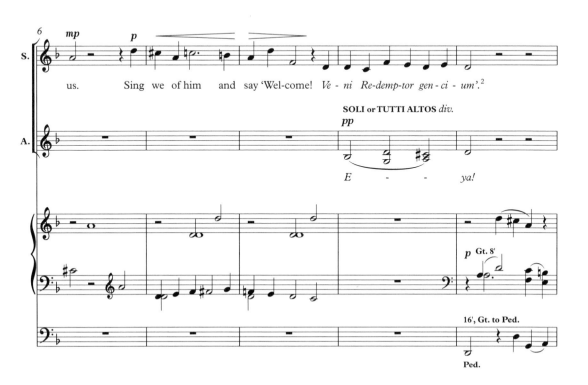

* There should be a continuous crescendo over the whole carol.

[1] The Only-begotten of the Father   [2] Come, Redeemer of the nations

[3]Let every age perceive (that)

[4] The high Word forthcoming   [5] From the rising of the sun

[8]Mary conceived in her womb

[9]Sharing in the light of his Father

[10]O Light of the Holy Trinity

S.1 - maid - en   free: Glo - ri - a,   glo - ri - a!_____

S.2 - maid - en   free: Glo - ri - a   ti - bi   Do - mi - ne![11]

A.   - maid - en   free: Glo - ri - a   ti - bi   Do - mi - ne![11]

T.   - maid - en   free: Glo - ri - a   ti - bi   Do - mi - ne![11]

B.   - maid - en   free: Glo - ri - a   ti - bi   Do - mi - ne![11]

[11] Glory to thee, O Lord!

for the Mormon Tabernacle Choir

7. Ding dong! merrily on high

G. R. Woodward
(1848–1934)

Melody: 16th-cent. French
arr. MACK WILBERG (b. 1955)
organ part by Peter Stevens

Gt. 8', 4'
Sw. 8', 4', 2', Mixt.
Ped. 16', 8'
Sw. to Gt.

Also available separately (ISBN 978–0–19–380486–9) and in a version for SATB and piano four-hands (ISBN 978–0–19–387049–9). Both these versions include extended interludes at bars 25 and 53, as does the orchestral accompaniment (see page ix).

The original organ version was first performed by the Choir of King's College, Cambridge, directed by Stephen Cleobury, with organist Peter Stevens, at the Festival of Nine Lessons and Carols on Christmas Eve 2007.

8. Blest Mary wanders through the thorn

trans. Hugh Keyte and Andrew Parrott

Trad. German
arr. STEPHEN CLEOBURY (b. 1948)

* Keyboard reduction for rehearsal only.

9. Carol

Norman Nicholson
(1914–87)

FRANCIS POTT
(b. 1957)

^{1}*miry* = boggy

and by   the   fire____ with - in____ His   limbs____   the   rest - ing   roots   were

roots____ were

Movendo di più

warm._____   3. Ma - ry   hid____   her__   Child__   be - tween_____

hil - locks_   of   hard____   sand;_____   by   sing - ing   wa   -   ter____

poco calando

in____   His____   veins____   grass   sprang_   from   the____   ground._____

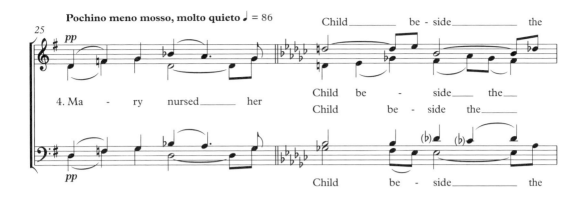

for John Romeri and the Church of the Assumption, Pittsburgh

10. Candlelight Carol

Words and music by
JOHN RUTTER (b. 1945)

how can you write down a baby's first cry?
Ma - ry will hold him and sing him to sleep.

S. Can-dle-light, an-gel light, fire - light and star - glow Shine on his

A. Can - dle - light, an-gel light and star - glow Shine on his

T. Can - dle - light, an-gel light and star - glow Shine on his

B. 1 Can - dle-light, an - gel light, fire - light and star-glow Shine on his

B. 2 Can - dle - light, fire - light and star-glow Shine on his

play in verse 2 only—verse 1 unaccompanied

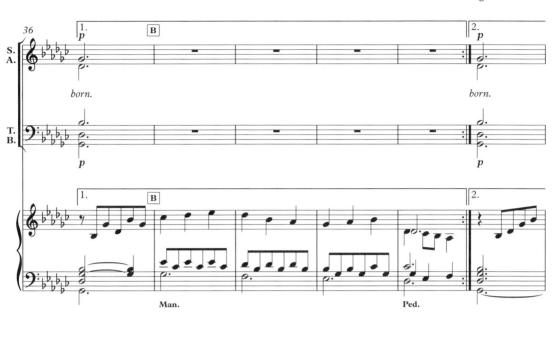

A child with his
God-head in - car - nate and hope__ of sal - va - tion:__ mm__
mo - ther that first Christ - mas Day.   *ah__
Can-dle-light, an-gel light,
fire - light and star - glow   Shine on his cra - dle till break - ing of

* or hum, at conductor's discretion

11. Glory to the Christ Child

Verse taken from BM Add. MS 29401 (*c.*1610)

ALAN BULLARD
(b. 1947)

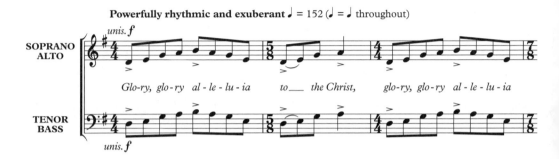

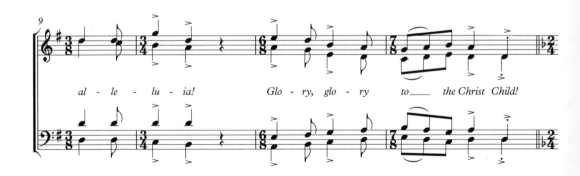

Also available separately (ISBN 978–0–19–335567–5).

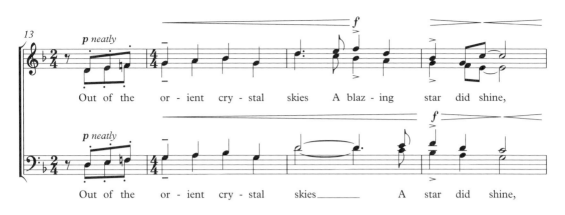

Out of the or - ient cry - stal skies A blaz - ing star did shine,

Out of the or - ient cry - stal skies_____ A star did shine,

Show - ing the place where sleep-ing lies__ A bless - ed babe di - vine.

Glo - ry, glo-ry al - le - lu - ia to__ the Christ, glo-ry, glo-ry al - le - lu - ia to__ the Christ Child!

Glo-ry, glo-ry al - le - lu - ia to__ the Christ Child, glo-ry al - le - lu - ia to__ the Christ Child!

Al - le - lu - ia! Glo - ry, glo - ry to__ the Christ, al - le - lu - ia!

Glo - ry, glo - ry to___ the Christ Child! This ve - ry star the kings did

guide, E'en from the fur - thest East,

guide, E'en from the East, To Beth - le-hem where it be - tide___ This

guide, E'en from the fur - thest East,

guide, E'en from the fur - thest East,

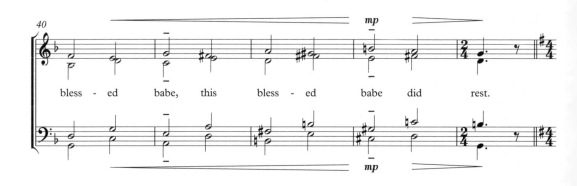

bless - ed babe, this bless - ed babe did rest.

Glo - ry, glo - ry al - le - lu - ia to___ the Christ, glo - ry, glo - ry al - le - lu - ia

Glo - ry, glo - ry al - le - lu - ia to___ the Christ Child, glo - ry al - le - lu - ia

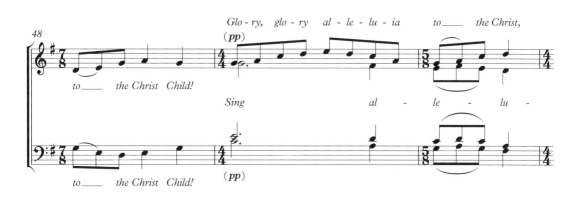

birth   A thou-sand an - gels sing:___ 'Glo-ry   and peace   un - to   the earth_ Where

birth   The   an - gels sing:

born   is   this   new   King,   this   new   King!'   Al -

King!'   Glo - ry,   glo-ry, glo-ry al - le - lu - ia

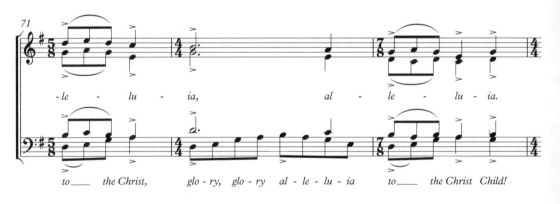

- le   -   lu   -   ia,   al   -   le   -   lu - ia.

to___   the Christ,   glo - ry, glo - ry al - le - lu - ia   to___   the Christ Child!

Glo-ry, glo - ry al - le - lu - ia   to___   the Christ,   glo - ry, glo - ry al - le - lu - ia

Sing   al   -   le   -   lu   -   ia,   al -

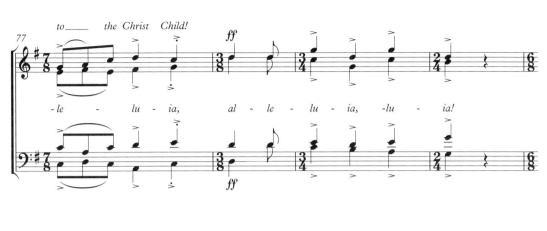

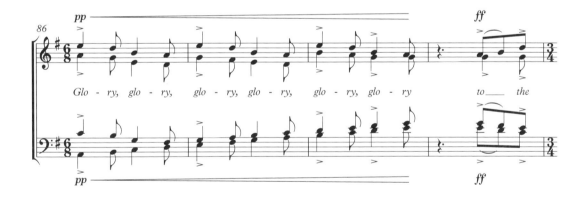

slower: intense and expressive

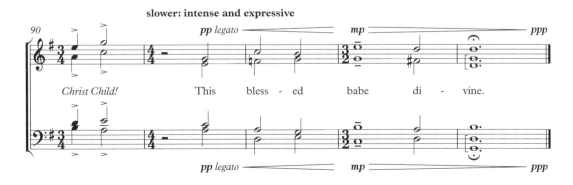

12. God rest you merry, gentlemen

Trad. English
arr. MARK SIRETT (b. 1952)

rest you mer-ry, gen-tle-men, Let no-thing you dis-may, For Je-sus Christ our

Sa - viour Was born up-on this day, To save us all from Sa-tan's power When

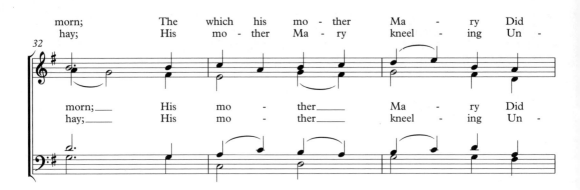

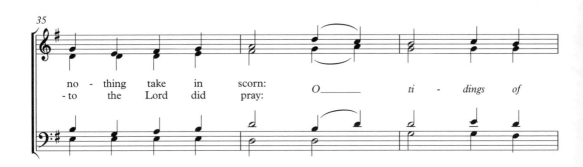

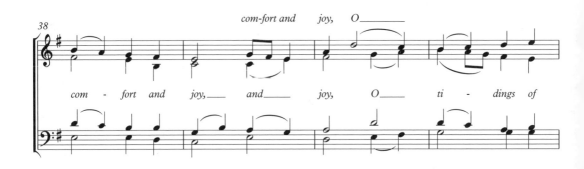

1st time to v. 3
on next page
2nd time to v. 6
on p. 61

3. From God our heav'n-ly Fa - ther A bless-ed an - gel came, And un - to cer - tain

shep - herds Brought ti - dings of the same, How that in Beth - le - hem was born The

Son of God by name: O___ ti - dings of com - fort and joy, com-fort and

joy, O___ ti - dings of com - fort and joy.___

TENORS & BASSES

4. The shep-herds at those ti - dings Re - joic - ed much in mind, And

left their flocks a - feed - ing In tem - pest, storm and wind, And

went to Beth - le - hem straight-way This bless - ed babe to find:

com-fort and joy, O_____

O_____ ti - dings of com - fort and joy,_____ and_____ joy, O_____

to v. 5 on p. 57

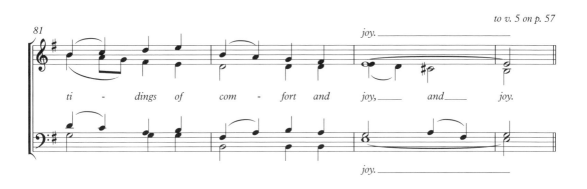

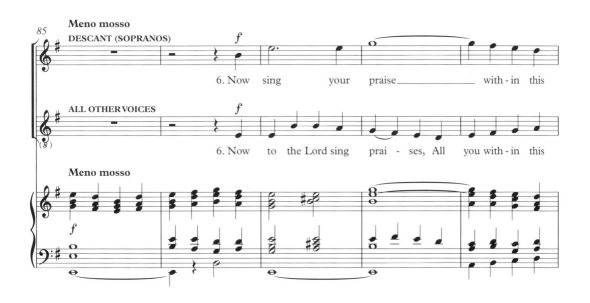

13. Good King Wenceslas

J. M. Neale
(1818–66)

Melody from *Piae Cantiones* (1582)
arr. BOB CHILCOTT (b. 1955)

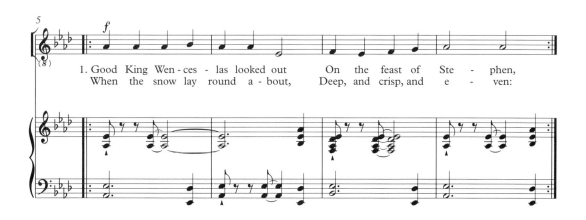

When a poor man came in sight, Ga-th'ring win-ter fu - - el.

Man.

mf 2. 'Hi - ther, page, and stand by me, If thou know'st it, tell - ing,
Yon - der pea-sant, who is he? Where and what his dwell - ing?'

unis. mf 'Sire, he lives a good league hence, Un - der-neath the

Ped.

-ge - ther: Through the rude wind's wild la - ment And the bit - ter

dim.

wea - ther. _____

Man.

unis. p

S./A.

4. 'Sire, the night is dark - er now, And the wind blows stron - ger;

p

Fails my heart, I know not how; I can go no lon - ger.'

14. Hush! my dear

Isaac Watts
(1674–1748)

GABRIEL JACKSON
(b. 1962)

1. Hush! my dear, lie still and slum - ber; Ho - ly
2. Soft and ea - sy is thy cra - dle, Coarse and
3. See the kind - ly shep - herds round him, Tell - ing
4. May'st thou live to know and fear him, Trust and

an - gels guard thy bed! Heav'n - ly bless - ings with - out
hard thy Sa - viour lay When___ his birth - place was a
won - ders from the sky! Where___ they sought him, there they
love him all thy days; Then___ go dwell for ev - er

num - ber Gent - ly fall - ing on thy head.___
sta - ble And___ his soft - est bed was hay.___
found him, With___ his Vir - gin Mo - ther by.___
near him, See___ his face___ and sing his praise!

Choirs may vary the dynamics and scoring between verses, for example sopranos with ATB vocalizing (*ah*, *mm*, *oo*, etc.), melody in unison with organ accompaniment, tenor solo with SATB vocalizing, etc.

15. Hark! the herald-angels sing

Charles Wesley (1707–88)
and others

FELIX MENDELSSOHN (1809–47)*
v. 3 arr. PAUL LEDDINGTON WRIGHT (b. 1951)

* Melody and harmony for verses 1 and 2 adapted by W. H. Cummings (1831–1915) from a chorus by Mendelssohn.

† Omit manual parts in bars 1–2 when performing with brass quintet.

© Oxford University Press 2011. Photocopying this copyright material is ILLEGAL.

17

With th'an - gel - ic   host pro - claim,   Christ is— born   in   Beth - le - hem.
Pleased as   man with   man   to dwell,   Je - sus,— our   Em - ma - nu - el.

21

Org.

Hark!   the he - rald - an - gels sing   Glo - ry— to   the   new - born King.

Org. Ped.

25 DESCANT (SOPRANOS)   *f*

3. Hail!   O hail the— Sun—   of   Right-eous - ness!

ALL OTHER VOICES   *f*

(8)
3. Hail   the heav'n - born Prince of   Peace!_   Hail   the   Sun   of   Right-eous - ness!

f

Ped.

29

Light   and life   to   all— he brings,   Ris'n with heal - ing   in   his— wings;

(8)
Light   and   life   to   all   he   brings,   Ris'n with heal - ing   in   his   wings;

16. I sing of a maiden

15th-cent. English

MATTHEW MARTIN
(b. 1976)

[1] *makeless* = matchless   [2] *ches* = chose

* Small notes optional.

First performed by the Choir of Merton College, Oxford, conducted by Benjamin Nicholas, on 2 December 2010.

[4]Godes = God's

17. I saw a stable

Mary Coleridge
(1861–1907)

ALAN BULLARD
(b. 1947)

I saw a sta - ble, low and ve - ry bare, A lit - tle child in a

man - ger._____ The ox - en knew him, had him in their care,____ A lit - tle child in a man - ger. The safe - ty of the world, the

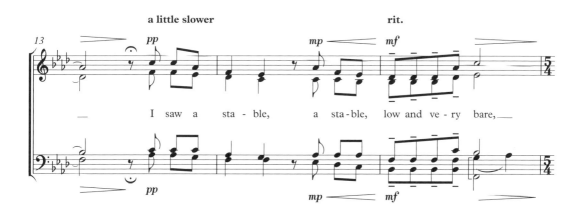

18. I saw three ships

Trad. English

ANDREW SIMPSON
(b. 1968)

Joyfully ♩ = 116

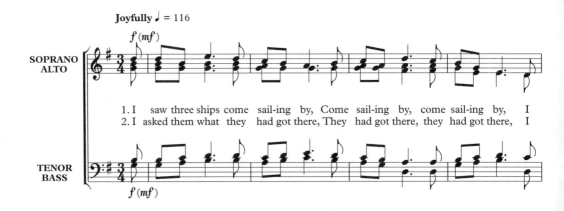

1. I saw three ships come sail-ing by, Come sail-ing by, come sail-ing by, I
2. I asked them what they had got there, They had got there, they had got there, I

saw three ships come sail-ing by At Christ-mas Day in the morn - ing.
asked them what they had got there At Christ-mas Day in the morn - ing.

3. They said they had____ a Sa-viour there,___ A Sa-viour there,___ a Sa-viour there,_

3. They said they had a Sa-viour there, A Sa-viour there, a Sa-viour there, They

They said they had ___ a Sa-viour there At Christ-mas Day in the morn-ing.

said they had a Sa-viour there At Christ-mas Day in the morn - ing.

S. SOLO

mp dolce

4. They washed his head in a gold-en bowl, In a gold-en bowl, in a gold-en bowl, They

S. A.

mm *mm*

p

mm *mm*

T. B.

p

mm

rit.   *slower*

washed his head in a gold-en bowl At Christ-mas Day in the morn - ing.

mm

mm

mm

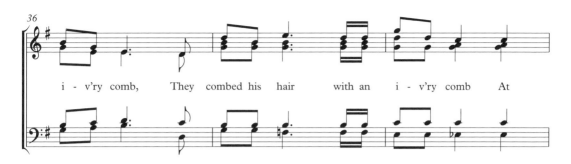

i - v'ry comb,   They   combed his   hair   with an   i - v'ry comb   At

Christ-mas Day   in the   morn - ing._____   7. And   all   the bells, and

morn - ing.   7. And   all   the bells,   and

all   the bells   in   heav'n did ring,   Heav'n did   ring,____   heav'n did ring,   To

think that Christ   was   born a king   At   Christ-mas Day   in the   morn - ing.

19. In dulci jubilo

English text translated from German
by R. L. Pearsall

Old German carol
arr. BOB CHILCOTT (b. 1955)

[1] In sweet jubilation   [2] In a manger

³In mother's lap. You are Alpha and Omega!   ⁴O infant Jesus!   ⁵O the best of boys!   ⁶O Prince of glory! Draw me after you!

(38)
unis. p

S./A.

3. O   Pa - tris ca - ri - tas,____   O   Na - ti le - ni - tas!⁷____   Deep - ly were we

p

Man.

44

poco cresc.

stain - ed *Per nos - tra cri - mi - na;*⁸____ But thou hast for us gain - ed *Coe - lo - rum gau - di -*

poco cresc.

50

mp cresc.   mf

S.
A.

- a.⁹____   O   that we   were   there,____   O   that we__ were   there!____

T.
B.

mp cresc.   mf

mp cresc.   mf

mp cresc.   mf

Ped.

⁷O love of the Father, O mercy of the Son!   ⁸Through our sins   ⁹The joys of heaven

[10]Where are the joys   [11]New songs   [12]In the king's courts

20. It came upon the midnight clear

E. H. Sears
(1810–76)

Trad. English
adap. and harm. ARTHUR SULLIVAN (1842–1900)
vv. 3 & 4 arr. JOHN SCOTT (b. 1956)

1. It— came u - pon the— mid-night clear, That glo -rious song of old, From
2. Still— through the clo - ven— skies they come, With peace-ful wings un - furled; And

an - gels bend - ing near the earth To— touch their harps of gold: 'Peace
still their heav'n - ly mu - sic floats— O'er— all— the— wea - ry world; A -

on the earth, good - will to men, From heav'n's all gra - cious King!' The
- bove its sad and low - ly plains They bend on ho - v'ring wing; And

world in___ so - lemn still - ness___ lay To___ hear___ the___ an - gels sing.
ev - er___ o'er its___ Ba - bel___ sounds The___ bless - ed___ an - gels sing.

*3. Yet___ with the___ woes of___ sin___ and___ strife The___ world has suf - fered

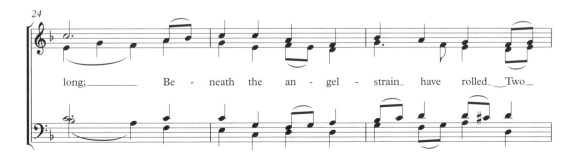

long;_____ Be - neath the an - gel - strain___ have rolled___ Two___

* Verse 3 may be sung unaccompanied.

21. It came upon the midnight clear

E. H. Sears
(1810–76)

Melody by RICHARD STORRS WILLIS (1819–1900)
arr. UZZIAH BURNAP (1834–1900)
vv. 3 & 4 arr. MACK WILBERG (b. 1955)

*3. Yet with the woes of sin and strife The world has suf - fered long;___ Be -

- neath the an - gel - strain have rolled Two thou - sand years___ of wrong;___ And

man, at war___ with man, hears not The love - song which they bring:___ O

hush the noise, ye men of strife, And hear___ the an - gels sing!___

* Verse 3 may be performed in four parts, with or without organ, or by unison voices with organ.

22. Joy to the world!

Isaac Watts
(1674–1748)

LOWELL MASON (1792–1872)
based on Handel
arr. MACK WILBERG (b. 1955)

The melody line may be sung in unison throughout.

ALL VOICES

4. He rules the world with truth and grace, And makes the na - tions prove The glo - ries___ of___ his

for John Rutter on his 60th birthday

23. Lullay, my liking

Anon. 15th cent.

DAVID WILLCOCKS
(b. 1919)

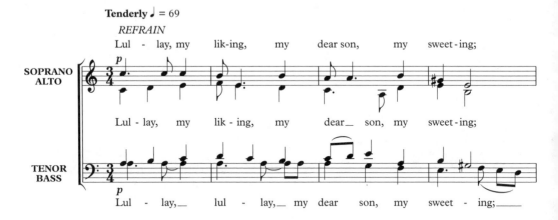

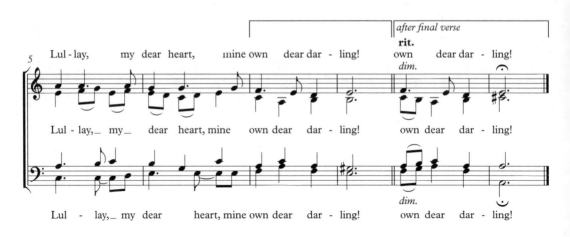

* Each verse may be sung by one or more upper-voice soloists, according to the resources of the choir.

Also available separately (ISBN 978-0-19-335559-0).

VERSE 2
SOLO *mp*

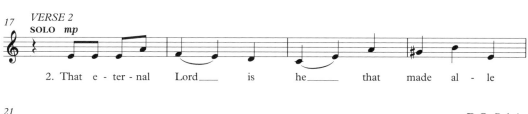

2. That e - ter - nal Lord___ is he___ that made al - le

D.C. *Refrain*

thing: Of al - le lord - es he is Lord, of al - le king - es King.

VERSE 3
SOLO   *mp*

3. There was mic - kle[1] me-lo-dy at that Child-es birth: Al - though

D.C. *Refrain*

they were in hea - ven's bliss they ma - de mic - kle mirth.

VERSE 4
SOLO   *mp*

4. An - gels bright they sang that night, and said - en to that Child:

D.C. *Refrain*

'Bless - ed be thou,___ and so be she___ that is both meek and mild!'

VERSE 5
SOLO
mp

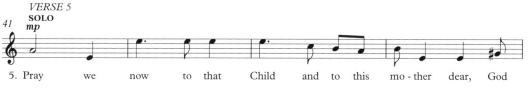

5. Pray we now to that Child and to this mo - ther dear, God

D.C. *Refrain*

grant them all his bless - ing that now mak - en cheer!

Optional ending: after the refrain following verse 5, the soloists may sing their verses simultaneously, with a final refrain sung *pp*.

[1]*mickle* = much

in memory of my mother, Marilyn

24. Lo, how a Rose e'er blooming

16th-cent. (vv. 1 & 2) and 19th-cent. (v. 3) German
trans. Theodore Baker (v. 1 adap.);
Catherine Winkworth, DB (v. 2); Harriet R. Spaeth (v. 3)

Melody: 14th-cent. German
arr. DAVID BLACKWELL (b. 1961)

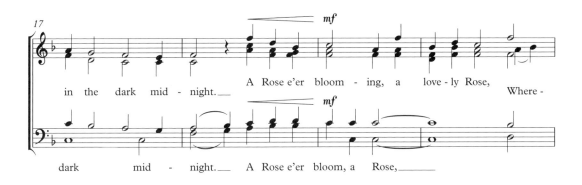

in the dark mid - night.___ A Rose e'er bloom - ing, a love - ly Rose, Where -

dark mid - night.___ A Rose e'er bloom, a Rose,_____

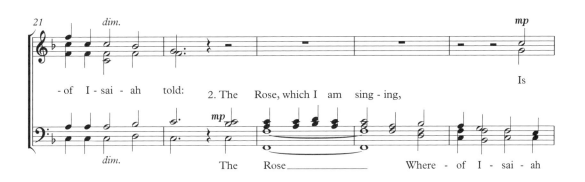

- of I - sai - ah told: 2. The Rose, which I am sing - ing,

Is

The Rose_____ Where - of I - sai - ah

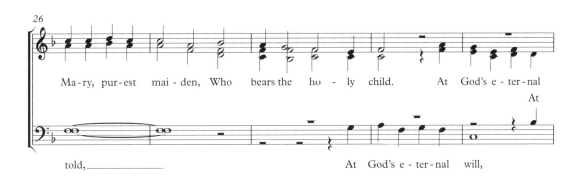

Ma - ry, pur - est mai - den, Who bears the ho - ly child. At God's e - ter - nal

At

told,_____ At God's e - ter - nal will,

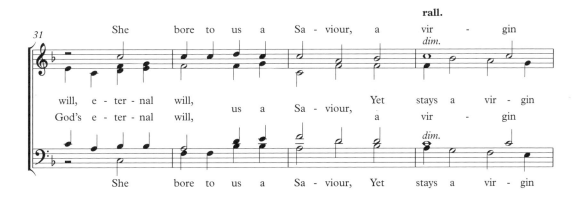

She bore to us a Sa - viour, a vir - gin

will, e - ter - nal will, us a Sa - viour, Yet stays a vir - gin
God's e - ter - nal will, a vir - gin

She bore to us a Sa - viour, Yet stays a vir - gin

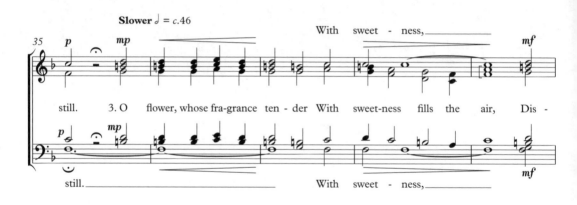

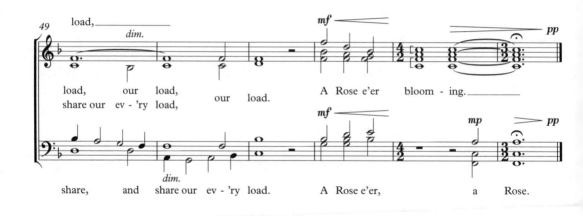

25. My Lord has Come

Words and music by
WILL TODD (b. 1970)

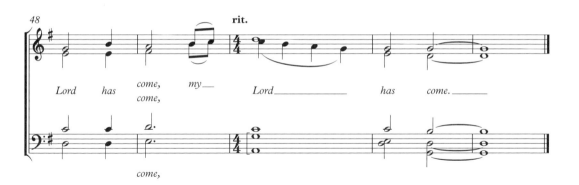

Commissioned by the Organist and Choir of Sandringham Church
in celebration of the 80th birthday year of HM The Queen.
First performed, in her presence, on New Year's Eve 2006

26. New Year

Words and music by
JOHN RUTTER (b. 1945)

Also available separately (ISBN 978–0–19–335939–0).

hope,   new   year,_____   New light,   new hope,   new

year._____

New   year._____

SOPRANOS & ALTOS

Turn your ears to the sound;   Some-where near, a voice is call-ing:

* Altos sing lower notes, at conductor's discretion.

Hear the news, Turn your ears to the sound.

TENORS & BASSES
mf dolce cantabile

Turn your heart to the love; Christ is come to bring the world new

life, to bring new life. The

voice is al-ways there,_____ if the world will hear it;_____

And

Ped.

27. O come, O come, Emmanuel

18th-cent. (or earlier) Latin,
based on the Advent Antiphons
trans. John Mason Neale

Melody: 15th-cent. French
adap. and arr. PAUL LEDDINGTON WRIGHT (b. 1951)

Verses 1, 2, 3, 6, and 7 follow the order of J. M. Neale's translation as used in most common hymnbooks and also the order of the original 5-verse Latin hymn-version. Verses 4 and 5 may be included using the repeats; these complete the sequence of 7 verses, though not in the original order of the antiphons. Verse 1 was originally the last antiphon, and may be repeated at the end.

-ma - nu - el shall come to thee, O Is - ra - el.

S./A.

unis. **mf**

3. O come, thou Day-spring, come_____ and cheer_____ our
5. O come, De - sire of na - tions, bring_____ all

mf

Man.

spi - rits by thine ad - vent here; dis - perse the gloom - y clouds_ of night, and
peo-ples to their Sa - viour King; thou Cor-ner-stone, who ma - kest one, com-

o - pen wide our heav'n - ly home; make safe the way that leads____ on high, and

close the path to mi - se - ry: Re - joice! Re - joice! Em -

- ma - nu - el shall come to thee, O Is - ra - el.

MOST VOICES

7. O   Come, O come, thou Lord____ of Might,   who

Ped.

* Lower parts of the descant may be omitted.

for Kate and Becky

28. O little town

Phillips Brooks
(1835–93)

BOB CHILCOTT
(b. 1955)

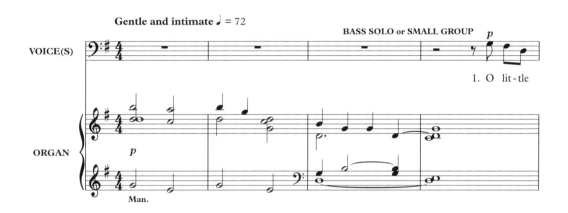

13

in   thy__ dark__ streets   shin - eth   The   ev - er - last - ing__

16

light;   The hopes and   fears   of   all   the   years__   Are met in

19

thee   to - night.

23

S./A.

unis. p

2. O morn-ing stars,   to - ge - ther__   Pro-claim the   ho - ly

T./B.

unis. pp

*oo__

Man.

Ped.

* Melody: Trad. English

sleep,   the   an-gels keep___ Their watch of won - d'ring love.

Man.

BASS SOLO or SMALL GROUP

3. How___   si - lent-ly, how

S.1

3. How   si - lent - ly, how

S.2 A.

*oo*___

T. B.

29. Old Christmas Returned (or Hospitality Revived)

Being a Looking-glass for rich Misers, wherein they may see (if they be not blind) how much they are to blame for their penurious house-keeping, and likewise an encouragement to those noble-minded gentry, who lay out a great part of their estates in hospitality, relieving such persons as have need thereof: 'Who feasts the poor, a true reward shall find, Or helps the old, the feeble, lame, and blind.'*

Anon.*

JAAKKO MÄNTYJÄRVI
(b. 1963)

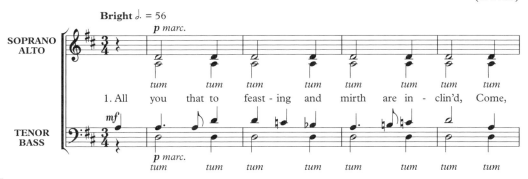

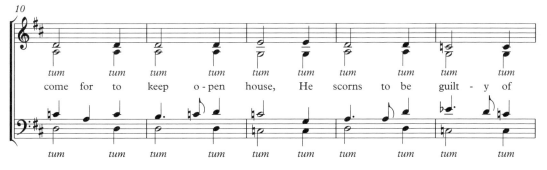

* From William Sandys, *Christmas Carols Ancient and Modern* (London, 1833).

chief, Plum - pud-ding, goose, ca-pon, minc'd pies and roast beef!

2. The times were ne'er good since Old Christ - mas was fled,___ And

2. The times ne'er good, Old Christ - mas fled, And

all hos-pi - ta - li - ty hath been so dead; No mirth at our

hos - pi - ta - li - ty be dead;___ No mirth of

fes - ti - vals late did ap - pear, They scarce - ly would part with a

late it did ap - pear, And they'd not part a

cup_ of March beer. But_ now you shall have, for the ease of your

grief, Plum - pud-ding, goose, ca-pon, minc'd pies and roast beef!

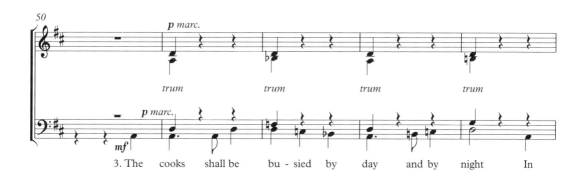

trum *trum* *trum* *trum*

3. The cooks shall be bu - sied by day and by night In

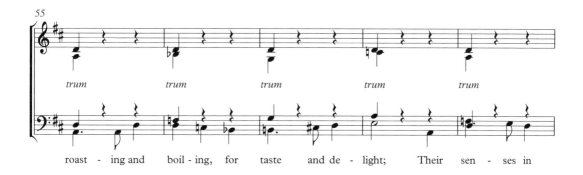

trum *trum* *trum* *trum* *trum*

roast - ing and boil-ing, for taste and de - light; Their sen - ses in

trum   trum   trum   trum   trum   trum

li-quor that's nap-py[1] they'll steep, Though they be af - ford - ed to

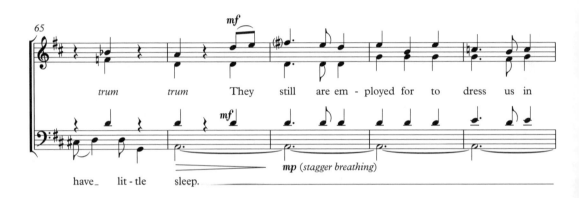

trum   trum   They still are em - ployed for to dress us in

have_ lit - tle sleep.

mp (stagger breathing)

brief,__ Plum - pud-ding, goose, ca-pon, minc'd pies and roast beef!

Roast beef!

*4. Then wel - come we Old Christ - mas, town, Who

4. Then well may we wel - come Old Christ - mas to town,__ Who

[1] *nappy* = strong, heady

* If *divisi* is possible, the 2nd sopranos should double the (tenor) melody in bars 75–91.

† Small notes optional.

30. O come, all ye faithful
(*Adeste, fideles*)

trans. F. Oakeley,
W. T. Brooke,
and others

Words and melody by
J. F. WADE (1711–86)
vv. 6 & 7 arr. PHILIP LEDGER (b. 1937)

The harmonies used for verses 1–5 are from *The English Hymnal*.

3. See how the shepherds,
   Summoned to his cradle,
Leaving their flocks, draw nigh with lowly fear;
   We too will thither
   Bend our joyful footsteps:
      O come, etc.

4. Lo! star-led chieftains,
   Magi, Christ adoring,
Offer him incense, gold, and myrrh;
   We to the Christ Child
   Bring our hearts' oblations:
      O come, etc.

5. Child, for us sinners
   Poor and in the manger,
Fain we embrace thee, with awe and love;
   Who would not love thee,
   Loving us so dearly?
      O come, etc.

31. Out of the orient crystal skies

Anon. 17th cent.

KERRY ANDREW
(b. 1978)

* The '-ti-' and '-di-' in *falantidingdido* should be pronounced as 'tie' and 'dye'.

[1]*hight* = was called   [2]*betide* = happened (that)

6. The

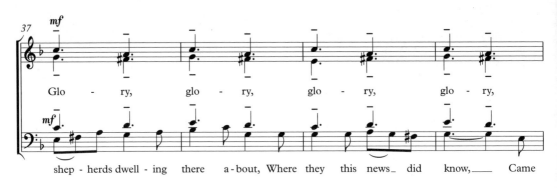

Glo - ry, glo - ry, glo - ry, glo - ry,

shep - herds dwell - ing there a - bout, Where they this news_ did know,___ Came

sing - ing, sing - ing, glo - ry.___

sing - ing all e'en in___ a rout[3], 'Fa - lan - ti - ding - di - do!'

Fa - lan - ti - ding - di - do, fa - lan - ti - ding - di - do,___ fa - lan - ti - ding - di -

fa - lan - ti - ding, fa -

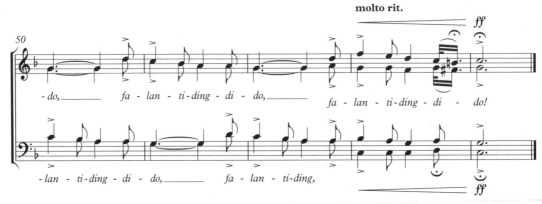

molto rit.

- do,___ fa - lan - ti - ding - di - do,___ fa - lan - ti - ding - di - do!

- lan - ti - ding - di - do,___ fa - lan - ti - ding,

[3]*rout* = a chaotic crowd

for Matthew Owens and Wells Cathedral Choir

32. Pilgrim Jesus

Kevin Crossley-Holland
(b. 1941)

BOB CHILCOTT
(b. 1955)

[1] Jesus! Christ! Jesus! Born!   [2] Body! Blessed! Pilgrim! Born!

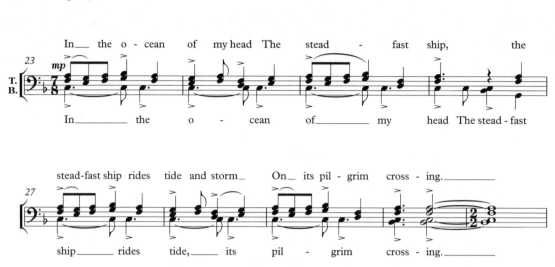

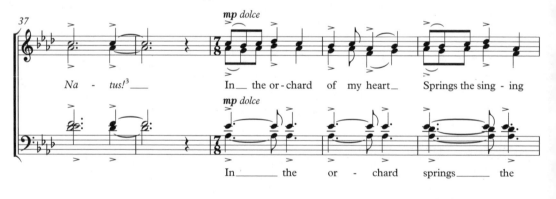

[3]Ocean! Pilgrim! Christ! Born!

33. Scots Nativity

Trad. Scottish

ALAN BULLARD
(b. 1947)

¹*bairn* = child

Also available separately (ISBN 978–0–19–343257–4) and in a version for SA and piano (ISBN 978–0–19–343256–7).

kind,   Shall   now____   re - joice____   both   heart____   and__

lov - ing,   Shall   now   re - joice____   both   heart   and

kind,   Shall   now____   re - joice____   both   heart   and

kind,____   Shall   now____   re - joice_   both   heart   and

poco tenuto   **a tempo**

mind;   Ba - low,   lam-my,   ba - loo - ba -

mind;   Ba - low,   lam-my,   ba - loo - ba -

mind;   Ba - low,   lam-my,   ba - loo - ba -

mind;   Ba - low,   lam-my,   ba - loo - ba -

poco tenuto   **a tempo**

² *Balow, lammy, baloobalow* = Sleep, my little lamb

34. See amid the winter's snow

Edward Caswall
(1814–78)

JOHN GOSS (1800–80)
arr. PAUL LEDDINGTON WRIGHT (b. 1951)

1. See a-mid the win-ter's snow, Born for us on earth be-low;
See the ten-der Lamb ap-pears, Pro-mis'd from e-ter-nal years:

Sing through all Je - ru - sa - lem, ___ Christ is born in Beth - le - hem.

DESCANT (SOPRANOS)
_oo_ ___ _aw_ ___

TENORS & BASSES _unis._
4. 'As we watch'd at dead of night, Lo, we saw a won - drous light;

_ah_ ___ Hail, _ thou_

An - gels sing - ing "Peace on earth" Told us of a Sa - viour's birth.'

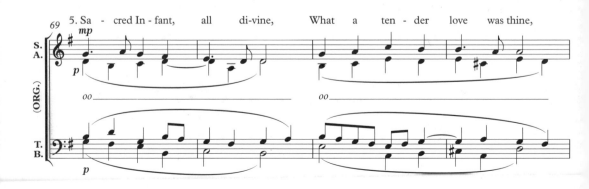

Thus to come from high-est bliss Down to such a world as this!

oo

Hail, thou ev-er-bless-ed morn! Hail, re-demp-tion's hap-py dawn!

Sing through all Je-ru-sa-lem, Christ is born in Beth-le-hem.

ALL VOICES

6. Teach, O teach us, Ho-ly Child, By thy face so meek and mild,

35. Silent night

Josef Mohr (1792–1848)
trans. John F. Young

FRANZ GRUBER (1787–1863)
arr. BOB CHILCOTT (b. 1955)

Gentle ♩ = 84

1. Si - lent night, ho - ly night, All is calm, all is bright; Round yon vir - gin mo - ther and child. Ho - ly in - fant so ten - der and mild, Sleep in hea - ven-ly peace, Sleep in hea - ven-ly peace.

2. Si - lent night,_ ho - ly night,_ Shep-herds first___ saw the sight:___

Glo - ries stream from heav'n_ a - far,___ Heav'n - ly hosts_ sing Al - le - lu -

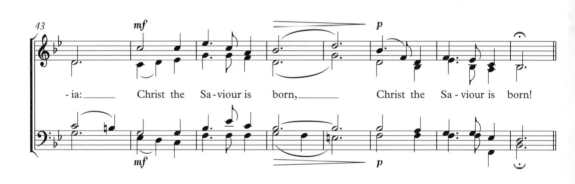

- ia:___ Christ the Sa - viour is born,___ Christ the Sa - viour is born!

DESCANT (SOPRANOS)

3. Si - lent_ night, ho - ly night, Son___ of___

ALL OTHER VOICES

3. Si - lent night, ho - ly night, Son of God,

Ped.

for David Lawrence and the City of Birmingham Young Voices

36. Sussex Carol

Trad. English
arr. BOB CHILCOTT (b. 1955)

in its place;   An - gels and   men with joy may   sing,___

S./A.

All   for   to see the   new-born   King.___

T./B.

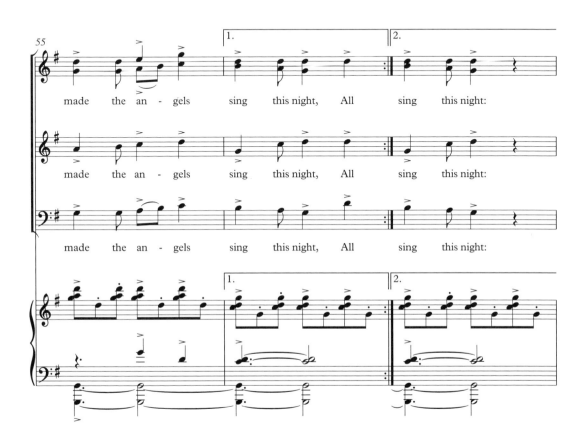

37. The Bell Carol

Henry Wadsworth Longfellow (adap.)
(1807–82)

PHILIP LEDGER
(b. 1937)

Joyfully ♩ = 108

f 1. I heard the bells on_ Christ-mas Day Their
mf 2. Till, ring - ing, sing-ing_ on its_ way, The

old_ fa - mi - liar_ ca - rols_ play, And mild_ and_ sweet the
world re - volved from_ night to_ day, A voice,_ a_ chime, a

words re - peat Of_ peace on_ earth this_ Christ - mas - tide.
chant sub - lime

loud and deep: 'God is not dead; nor does he sleep! The wrong shall fail, the right prevail, With peace on earth this Christ - mas - tide, this Christ - mas - tide.'

for Nick and Jane Wilson

38. The holly and the ivy

Trad. English

MATTHEW OWENS
(b. 1971)

SOPRANOS 1. The
TENORS 2. The
*SOPRANOS 3. The
*TENORS 4. The
SOPRANOS 5. The

1. hol - ly and the i - vy When they are both full grown; Of__ all the trees that are in the wood The hol - ly bears the crown.
2. hol - ly bears a blos - som As white as a - ny flower; And__ Ma - ry bore sweet Je - sus Christ To be our sweet Sa - viour.
3. hol - ly bears a ber - ry As red as a - ny blood; And__ Ma - ry bore sweet Je - sus Christ To do poor sin - ners good.
4. hol - ly bears a prick - le As sharp as a - ny thorn; And__ Ma - ry bore sweet Je - sus Christ On Christ-mas Day in the morn.
5. hol - ly bears a bark___ As bit - t'r as a - ny gall; And__ Ma - ry bore sweet Je - sus Christ For to re - deem us all.

* Verses 3 and 4 may be performed as solos, if desired.

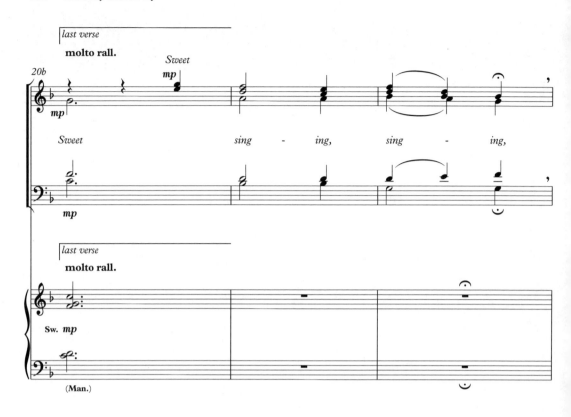

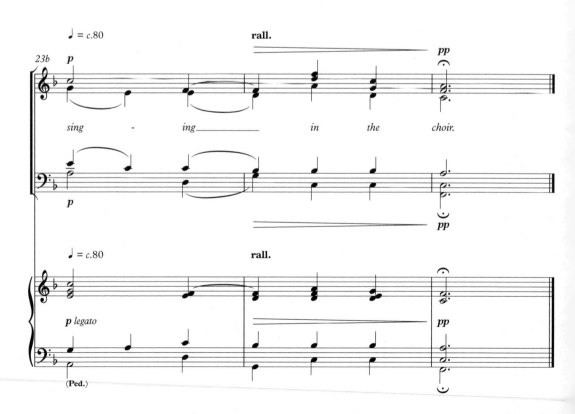

Commissioned by King's College, Cambridge

39. The Christ-child

G. K. Chesterton
(1874–1936)

GABRIEL JACKSON
(b. 1962)

First performed by the Choir of King's College, Cambridge, directed by Stephen Cleobury, on Christmas Eve 2009.

Also available separately (ISBN 978–0–19–336936–8).

© Oxford University Press 2010. Photocopying this copyright material is ILLEGAL.

here is   all__ a - right.)__

The   Christ-child lay   on Ma - ry's   breast,__   His   hair   was like a

Commissioned by the Friends of Harrow School for Harrow School Chapel Choir

40. The Sparrows' Carol

Charles Bennett
(b. 1954)

BOB CHILCOTT
(b. 1955)

* If performing on piano, play bass notes up an octave in bars 65, 67, and 69.

Winner of the Waverley Care Carol Competition, 2010

41. The Virgin's Song

15th cent. (adap.)

HERMIONE ROFF
(b. 1947)

¹*bere* = bier ²*fere* = companions

42. There is no rose

Anon. 15th cent.
adap. Alison Golding

HOWARD SKEMPTON
(b. 1947)

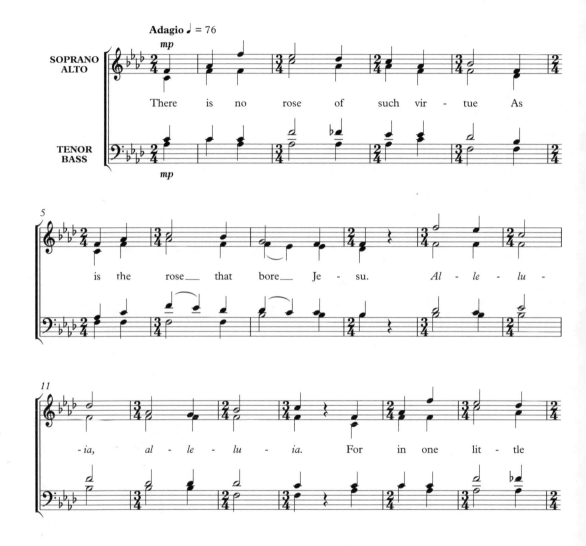

SOPRANO
ALTO

There is no rose of such vir - tue As
is the rose___ that bore___ Je - su. Al - le - lu -
- ia, al - le - lu - ia. For in one lit - tle
space this rose Could all of hea - ven and earth___ en - close.

TENOR
BASS

43. There is no rose

Anon. 15th cent.

ALAN SMITH
(b. 1962)

* Keyboard reduction for rehearsal only.

[1]A wonderful thing

²Of equal form   ³Glory to God in the highest   ⁴Let us rejoice

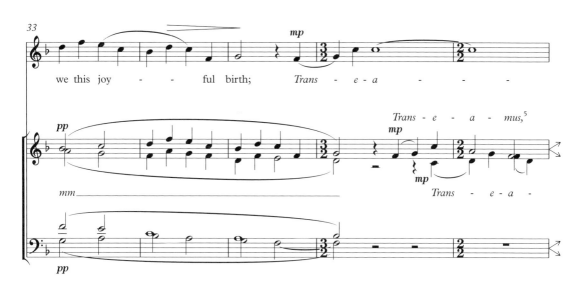

[5]Let us go

44. There's a song in the air!

Josiah G. Holland
(1819–81)

JOHN HEARNE
(b. 1937)

1. There's a song in the air! There's a star in the sky! There's a mo-ther's deep prayer and a ba-by's low cry! And the star rains its fire while the beau-ti-ful sing, For the man-ger of Beth-le-hem cra-dles a King!

2. There's a tu-mult of joy o'er the won-der-ful birth, For the vir-gin's sweet

boy is the Lord of__ the__ earth. Ay! the star rains its__ fire while the beau - ti-ful

sing, For the man - ger of Beth - le - hem__ cra - dles a King!_____

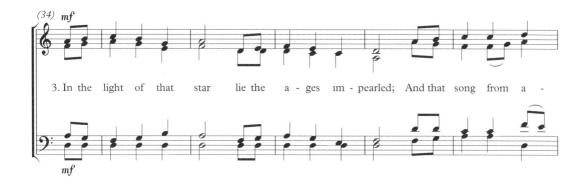

3. In the light of that star lie the a - ges im - pearled; And that song from a -

-far has swept o - ver__ the__ world. Ev-'ry hearth is a - flame, and the beau - ti-ful

sing   In the homes of   the   na - tions that_   Je - sus   is   King!_____

light,   and we   e - cho   the   song   That comes

4. We re - joice in   the_ light, and   we_   e - cho the song That   comes

down through the

4. We re - joice,_   and we   e - cho   the_   song That   comes

4. We re - joice, and_ we   e - cho the song That comes

night from the   hea - ven - ly throng. Ay! we shout to_ the_ love - ly e - van - gel they_

bring,   And we greet in   his   cra - dle   our_   Sa - vior and   King!_____

for Aubrey and Brittany

45. This endris night

15th-cent. English (adap.)

Z. RANDALL STROOPE
(b. 1953)

[1] *endris* = other

'My son, my bro - ther, fa - ther, dear, Why do you lie in bed of hay?'

'Ma - ry mo - ther,

ALTOS 'I am your child, Though I be laid

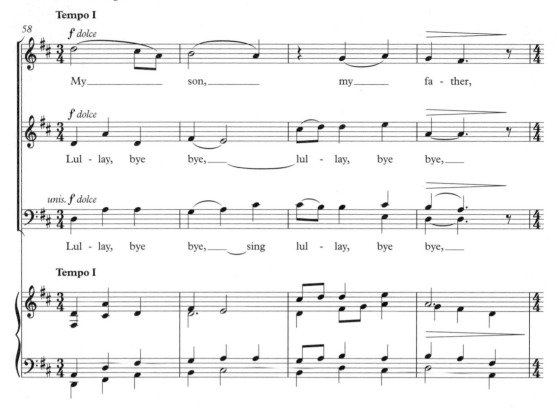

46. We three kings of Orient are

Words and melody by
JOHN HENRY HOPKINS (1820–91)
arr. PAUL LEDDINGTON WRIGHT (b. 1951)

star   of won - der,   star__ of night,__   Star   with roy - al   beau - ty bright,__

West - ward lead - ing,   still__ pro - ceed - ing, Guide us   to   thy   per - fect light.

cresc.   *ff*

27

unis. *f*

2. Born a king on Beth-le-hem plain, Gold I bring, to crown him a-gain,

mf

31 *unis.* *f*

King for ev - er, ceas - ing ne - ver, O - ver us all to reign: O____

f

35

star of won - der, star__ of night,__ Star with roy - al beau - ty bright,__

Prayer and prais-ing, all men rais-ing, Wor-ship him, God most high: O____

star of won-der, star__ of night,__ Star with roy - al beau-ty bright,__

West-ward lead - ing, still__ pro-ceed - ing, Guide us to thy per - fect light.

4. Myrrh is mine; its bit-ter per-fume___ Breathes a life of ga-ther-ing gloom;

ah___

Sor - r'wing, sigh - ing, bleed - ing, dy - ing, Sealed in the stone - cold

47. Voices in the Mist

Alfred, Lord Tennyson
(1809–92)

JUSSI CHYDENIUS
(b. 1972)

if a_ door Were shut be-tween me and the sound. Each voice four chan - ges

wind That now di - late,

on_ the wind____ That now di - late, and now de - crease,

That now di - late,_____ and now de-crease,

man -

Peace and good - will, good - will and peace,_ peace_ and good-will to all_ man -

Peace and_ good-will, good-will and peace,_

Peace and good - will, good - will and peace,

- kind, peace_____ to all_ man - kind.

rit.

- kind,_____ peace and good - will to all_ man - kind.

for the Portsmouth Choral Union

48. Wassail

Trad. English

JONATHAN WILLCOCKS
(b. 1953)

good   Christ-mas pie____   as   e'er__ I   did see;   With the   Was - sail-ing bowl__ we'll

drink   to   thee.   Was-sail,   was - sail.____

3. So

here's to the cow   and to   her broad horn, May   God send our mas - ter a   good crop of corn, And a

good crop of corn__ that we__ all may see; With the Was - sail-ing bowl we'll drink__ to

Was - sail, was - sail, was - sail,_ was - sail._____

Was-sail,_____ was-sail._____

4. Then

thee._____ Was - sail,_____ was - sail._____

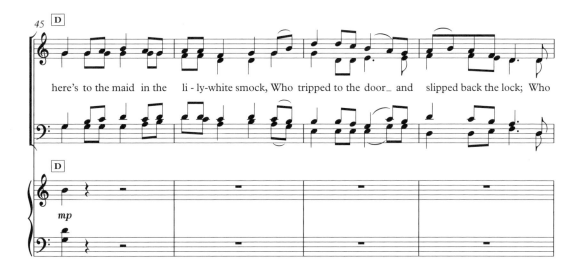

here's to the maid in the li - ly-white smock, Who tripped to the door_ and slipped back the lock; Who

tripped to the door__ and pulled back the pin For to let these jol - ly Was - sail - ers

Was-sail,   was - sail.__

in.

Was - sail,   was - sail.__

Was-sail,   was - sail.__

Was - sail,   was - sail.__

E

DESCANT (SOPRANOS)

(56)

5. Come but - ler,__ fill us a bowl; Then we hope your

ALL OTHER VOICES

(8)

5. Come but - ler, come fill us a bowl of the best; Then we hope that your soul__ in

E

49. While shepherds watched their flocks

Nahum Tate
(1652–1715)

Este's Psalter (1592)
v. 6 arr. BOB CHILCOTT (b. 1955)

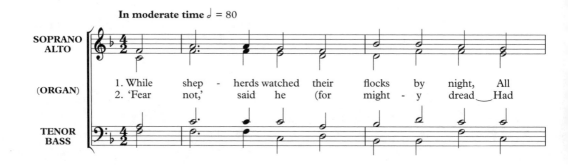

1. While shep - herds watched their flocks by night, All
2. 'Fear not,' said he (for might - y dread Had

seat - ed on the ground, The an - gel of the
seized their troub - led mind); 'Glad ti - dings of great

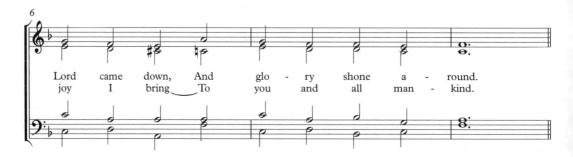

Lord came down, And glo - ry shone a - round.
joy I bring To you and all man - kind.

3. 'To you in David's town this day
   Is born of David's line
A Saviour, who is Christ the Lord;
   And this shall be the sign:

4. 'The heav'nly Babe you there shall find
   To human view displayed,
All meanly wrapped in swathing bands,
   And in a manger laid.'

5. Thus spake the seraph; and forthwith
   Appeared a shining throng
Of angels praising God, who thus
   Addressed their joyful song:

to Geoffrey Webber and the Choir of Gonville and Caius College, Cambridge

50. What child is this?

William Chatterton Dix
(1837–98)

THOMAS HEWITT JONES
(b. 1984)

child is this who, laid to rest, On Ma - ry's lap is sleep - ing? Whom
lies he in such mean es - tate, Where ox and ass are feed - ing? Good

an - gels greet with an-thems sweet, While shep-herds watch are keep - ing?
Christ-ians fear: for sin - ners here The si - lent Word is plead - ing.

This, this is Christ the King, Whom shep-herds wor - ship and an - gels sing:＿
Nails, spear shall pierce him through, The Cross be borne＿ for me,＿ for you:＿

Haste, haste to bring him praise, The Babe, the Son＿＿ of＿ Ma - ry.
Hail! hail the Word Made Flesh, The Babe, the Son＿＿ of＿

Ma - ry.

3. So

Man.

bring him in - cense, gold and myrrh; Come, peas-ant, king, to own_ him!_ The

King of Kings sal - va - tion brings: Let_ lov-ing hearts en - throne him!

Ped.

Raise, raise the song on high! The Vir-gin sings her lul - la - by.

Joy! joy! for Christ is born, The babe, the Son of Ma - ry!

S. SOLO

SOPRANO SOLO *mp espress.*

What

Man.

A FESTIVAL OF NINE LESSONS AND CAROLS

Below is a list of the traditional readings for the service of nine lessons and carols. It serves as a suggestion for the service order, but many may choose to reduce or increase the number of readings, or to change the selection, depending on the style or interpretation of the service they have chosen.

FIRST LESSON   God tells sinful Adam that he has lost the life of Paradise and that his seed will bruise the serpent's head.

Genesis 3: 8–15

SECOND LESSON   God promises to faithful Adam that in his seed shall all the nations of the earth be blessed.

Genesis 22: 15–18

THIRD LESSON   The prophet foretells the coming of the Saviour.

Isaiah 9: 2, 6–7

FOURTH LESSON   The peace that Christ will bring is foreshown.

Isaiah 11: 1–4 (to 'meek of the earth'), 6–9

FIFTH LESSON   The angel Gabriel salutes the Blessed Virgin Mary.

St Luke 1: 26–35, 38

SIXTH LESSON   St Luke tells of the birth of Jesus.

St Luke 2: 1, 3–7

ALTERNATIVE SIXTH LESSON   St Matthew tells of the birth of Jesus.

St Matthew 1: 18–23

SEVENTH LESSON   The shepherds go to the manger.

St Luke 2: 8–16

EIGHTH LESSON   The wise men are led by the star to Jesus.

St Matthew 2: 1–11

NINTH LESSON   St John unfolds the great mystery of the Incarnation.

St John 1: 1–14